Honeymoon Travel Journal

Copyright © 2021 by SHAW designs publishing
All rights reserved

Time is very slow for those who wait.
Very fast for those who are scared.
Very long for those who lament.
Very short for those who celebrate.
But for those who love, time is eternal.

William Shakespeare

Part 1: Planning

Together is our favorite place to be.

Notes

 # Honeymoon Information

Destination

Travel Dates

Travel Times

Lodging Information

Confirmation Numbers

Rental Car

Airplane Tickets

Lodging

Notes

Notes

Packing List

Packing List

☐	☐
☐	☐
☐	☐
☐	☐
☐	☐
☐	☐
☐	☐
☐	☐
☐	☐
☐	☐
☐	☐
☐	☐
☐	☐
☐	☐
☐	☐
☐	☐
☐	☐
☐	☐
☐	☐
☐	☐
☐	☐

Packing List

Packing List

Things We're Excited to Do

Notes

Part 2: Honeymooning

Married and in-love.
Let's celebrate, but this time
just the two of us!

Let the honeymoon begin...

Itinerary – Day 1

Morning

Afternoon

Evening

Memories - Day 1

Itinerary – Day 2

Morning

Afternoon

Evening

Memories – Day 2

Itinerary – Day 3

Morning

Afternoon

Evening

Memories – Day 3

Itinerary – Day 4

Morning

Afternoon

Evening

Memories - Day 4

Itinerary – Day 5

Morning

Afternoon

Evening

Memories – Day 5

Itinerary – Day 6

Morning

Afternoon

Evening

Memories – Day 6

Itinerary – Day 7

Morning

Afternoon

Evening

Memories - Day 7

Itinerary – Day 8

Morning

Afternoon

Evening

Memories – Day 8

Itinerary – Day 9

Morning

Afternoon

Evening

Memories – Day 9

Part 3: Reflecting

Marriage is more than love and fun, but our honeymoon had a lot of both!!

Favorites

Reflections

Additional Notes

Our honeymoon is over.

But the true adventure has only just begun.

Made in United States
North Haven, CT
05 October 2023